Diary of a Stepkid:

A Guided Journal for Tweens and Teens

by Wendy Lipscomb Deppe

Diary of a Stepkid: A Guided Journal for Tweens and Teens

ISBN - 1450573983

EAN - 9781450573986

Printed in the United States of America

Dear Stepkids,

It's hard enough to be a kid these days, and life gets even harder when your parents are divorced, and you become a stepkid! I know from experience: my parents got divorced when I was 11, and my mom remarried when I was 15. I was really angry and upset when my family split up, and although he seemed like a nice guy I *really* didn't want a stepdad! As it turned out, my stepdad ended up being such a wonderful guy that he legally adopted me. Our relationship wasn't always perfect, but I am so glad he is in my life.

Now I am a stepmom myself, and I see blended families in a whole new way. I know how hard things can be for kids of divorce because not only did I go through it myself, but I also see how it affects my stepkids.

One thing I have learned over the years is how helpful it can be to write my feelings down. When I am angry, upset, or sad, somehow getting it all out on paper helps get it off my chest. The thing is, no one ever told me this as a kid, and even if they had I wouldn't have known where to start!

I wrote this diary in hopes that it will help stepkids everywhere learn how to put their feelings on paper, and then maybe the feelings won't be so overwhelming. You can use the prompts to help you get started, and write about all the feelings you have: good, bad, and ugly. Keep the journal private, or you can choose to share it with your family members. I hope that this diary will help you to feel better about your life in a blended family. Happy journaling!

This journal belongs to

_____

For my eyes only!

My Life

Before my parents got divorced...

_____

_____

_____

_____

_____

_____

I enjoyed this about my family...

_____

_____

_____

_____

_____

 When my parents didn't get along I felt...

_____

_____

_____

_____

_____

My memories of the time my parents were still together...

_____

_____

_____

_____

_____

My Parents' Divorce

When my parents told me they were getting divorced, I felt...

_____

_____

_____

_____

When my parents separated...

_____

_____

_____

_____

During the divorce, this was hard on me...

_____

_____

_____

_____

_____

Other kids I knew whose parents are divorced, and what they told me...

_____

_____

_____

_____

_____

The worst part of my parents' divorce was...

_____

_____

_____

_____

_____

Something positive I can say about having divorced parents...

_____

_____

_____

_____

_____

My Parents' Remarriage

When my dad starting dating I felt...

_____

_____

_____

_____

_____

I didn't like my dad's girlfriend because...

_____

_____

_____

_____

_____

What I liked about my dad's girlfriend...

_____

_____

_____

_____

Things we did together...

_____

_____

_____

_____

When my dad told me he was getting married...

_____

_____

_____

_____

_____

My dad's wedding...

_____

_____

_____

_____

_____

When my mom started dating I felt...

_____

_____

_____

_____

_____

I didn't like my mom's boyfriend because...

_____

_____

_____

_____

_____

What I liked about my mom's boyfriend...

_____

_____

_____

_____

_____

Things we did together...

_____

_____

_____

_____

_____

When my mom told me she was getting married...

_____

_____

_____

_____

My mom's wedding...

_____

_____

_____

_____

My Dad

I love my dad because...

_____

_____

_____

_____

_____

Things I enjoy doing with my dad...

_____

_____

_____

_____

_____

Qualities I admire in my dad...

_____

_____

_____

_____

_____

Things that make it hard for me and my dad to get along...

_____

_____

_____

_____

_____

What I appreciate most about my dad...

_____

_____

_____

_____

_____

What I wish my dad could change is...

_____

_____

_____

_____

_____

My Mom

 I love my mom because...

_____

_____

_____

_____

_____

Things I enjoy doing with my mom...

_____

_____

_____

_____

Qualities I admire in my mom...

_____

_____

_____

_____

Things that make it hard for me and my mom to get along...

_____

_____

_____

_____

What I appreciate most about my mom...

_____

_____

_____

_____

What I wish my mom could change is...

_____

_____

_____

_____

My Stepdad

 I love my stepdad because...

_____

_____

_____

_____

Things I enjoy doing with my stepdad...

_____

_____

_____

_____

Qualities I admire in my stepdad...

_____

_____

_____

_____

_____

Things that make it hard for me and my stepdad to get along...

_____

_____

_____

_____

_____

What I appreciate most about my stepdad...

_____

_____

_____

_____

_____

_____

What I wish my stepdad could change is...

_____

_____

_____

_____

My Stepmom

I love my stepmom because...

_____

_____

_____

_____

_____

Things I enjoy doing with my stepmom...

_____

_____

_____

_____

_____

Qualities I admire in my stepmom...

_____

_____

_____

_____

_____

_____

Things that make it hard for me and my stepmom to get along...

_____

_____

_____

_____

What I appreciate most about my stepmom...

_____

_____

_____

_____

_____

_____

What I wish my stepmom could change is...

_____

_____

_____

_____

_____

My Siblings
and
Stepsiblings

These are my siblings...

_____

_____

_____

_____

These are my stepsiblings...

_____

_____

_____

_____

My siblings/stepsiblings and I fight about...

_____

_____

_____

_____

What I love most about my siblings/stepsiblings...

_____

_____

_____

_____

What drives me crazy about my siblings/stepsiblings...

_____

_____

_____

_____

_____

_____

My siblings/stepsiblings and I talk
about...

_____

_____

_____

_____

Things I enjoy doing with my siblings/stepsiblings...

_____

_____

_____

_____

When I grow up I want my relationship with them to be...

_____

_____

_____

_____

My Pets

These are the pets that I have...

_____

_____

_____

_____

_____

_____

I love my pets because...

_____

_____

_____

_____

My responsibilities for my pets...

_____

_____

_____

_____

_____

If I could make a wish for another pet it would be...

_____

_____

_____

_____

My Homes

These are the houses where I live...

_____

_____

_____

_____

The hardest thing about switching back and forth between houses is...

_____

_____

_____

_____

What I like most about my dad's house...

_____

_____

_____

_____

_____

_____

My least favorite thing about my dad's house...

_____

_____

_____

_____

What I like most about my mom's house...

_____

_____

_____

_____

_____

My least favorite things about my mom's house...

_____

_____

_____

_____

_____

My chores at my homes are...

_____

_____

_____

_____

_____

If I could change one thing about my homes it would be...

_____

_____

_____

_____

_____

My School

 My school is...

_____

_____

_____

_____

The subject I like the most is...

_____

_____

_____

_____

What I like best about school...

_____

_____

_____

_____

_____

What I like least about school...

_____

_____

_____

_____

My favorite teacher...

_____

_____

_____

_____

_____

The worst teacher...

_____

_____

_____

_____

My Friends

My friends are...

_____

_____

_____

_____

_____

My BEST friend is...

_____

_____

_____

_____

 My friends and I disagree about...

_____

_____

_____

_____

The ways my friends support me when I am having problems...

_____

_____

_____

_____

_____

I love to do these things with my friends...

_____

_____

_____

_____

_____

Spending time with my friends is important to me because...

_____

_____

_____

_____

My Activities

I am involved in...

_____

_____

_____

_____

_____

_____

If I could choose any hobby to learn more about it would be...

_____

_____

_____

_____

_____

Sports...

_____

_____

_____

_____

My activities make me happy because...

_____

_____

_____

_____

The thing that helps me relax the most...

_____

_____

_____

_____

_____

_____

I like to read...

_____

_____

_____

_____

A new activity I might want to try is...

_____

_____

_____

_____

_____

I am good at...

_____

_____

_____

_____

My Life Now

Now that my parents have been divorced for a while...

_____

_____

_____

_____

_____

What I enjoy about both sets of my family...

_____

_____

_____

_____

_____

I feel...

_____

_____

_____

_____

_____

_____

Now my life is like...

_____

_____

_____

_____

If I could change anything about my life it would be...

_____

_____

_____

_____

_____

My dreams for my future...

_____

_____

_____

_____

The best part of my life...

_____

_____

_____

_____

Other stuff...

_____

_____

_____

_____

About the author

Wendy is an administrator at a private school for children with learning disabilities. She lives in Texas with her husband, stepkids, and menagerie of dogs, cats, and fish. She is a regular contributor to StepMom Magazine. Wendy welcomes comments at stepmomscrapbook@gmail.com and invites you to read her blog at http://stepinthetrenches.blogspot.com.

To Pakapurk